Blues with a Butter Knife

The Unstoppable Music of CeDell Davis

Jason Peterson

illustrated by R. Gregory Christie

CALKINS CREEK
AN IMPRINT OF ASTRA BOOKS FOR YOUNG READERS
New York

"It just came to me when I was a kid. . . . I could do almost everything that you could do with your hands—I could do it with the knife. . . . It's all in the way you handle it. Drag, slide, push it up and down. If there's anybody else that sounds like me, I don't know. Never met nobody could do what I did."

Sometimes music cuts like a knife.
It did for young CeDell Davis.
The blues—the deep-down, stir-your-heart,
rattle-your-bones blues.

It surrounded him in the Arkansas and Mississippi Delta.
It rang out from the stage of his Daddy's juke joint.
It blasted from his cousin's record player on evenings after school or long days working the farm.
CeDell and his best bud Ike Ross grooving to the soulful sounds—cutting straight to his heart.

CeDell wanted to create this music he loved—but he had no instrument to play.

That is, until his cousin told him to pick peas one night for dinner.

Down in the dirt, he found a sonic surprise.

A harmonica. Beautiful in its dusty way and ready to be played.

CeDell chased a trail of notes, blowin' in the breeze.

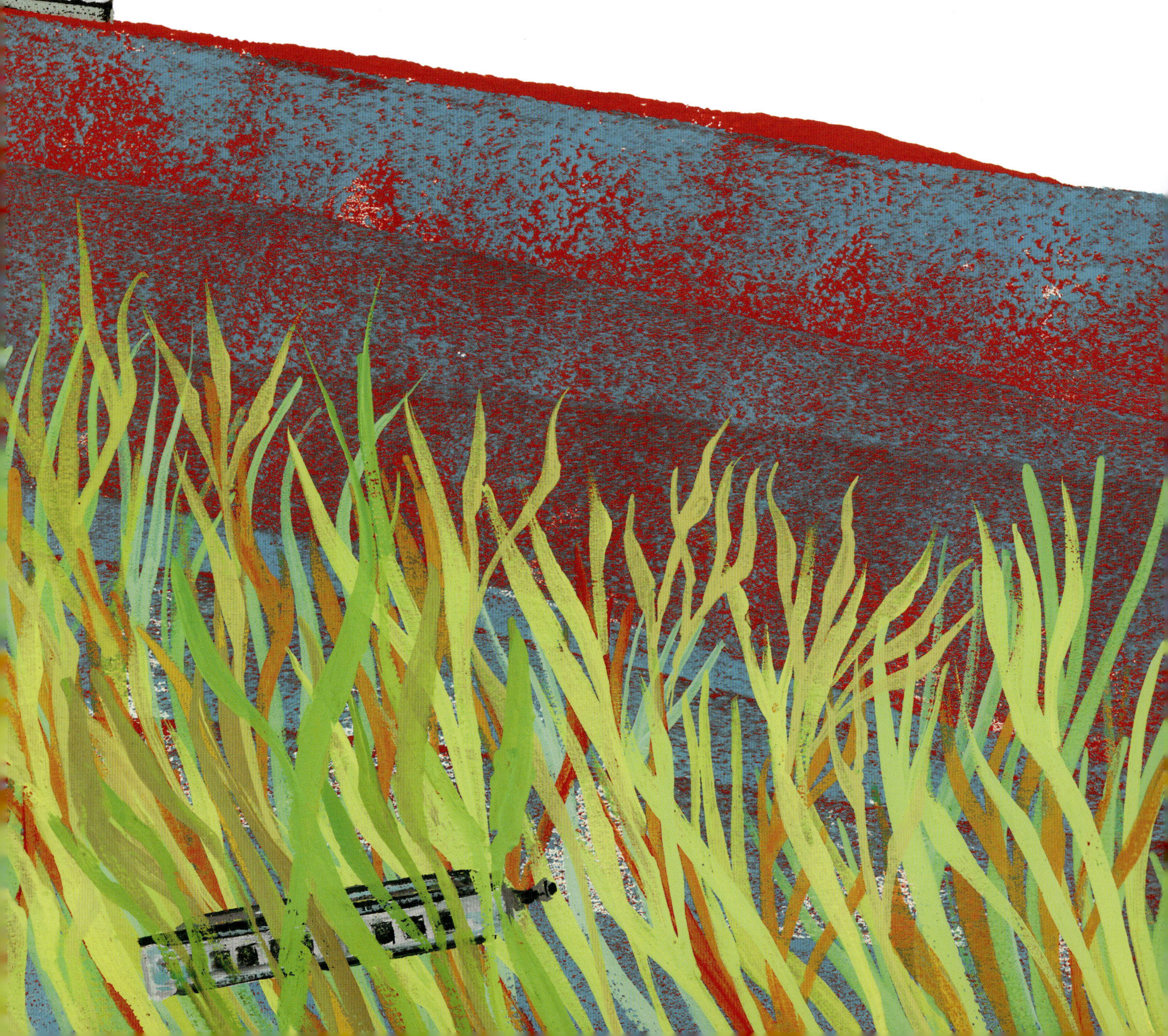

Next came a homemade diddley bow.

CeDell unwound the wire wrapping the bristles of his mother's broom.

He hammered one nail up high, and another down low—right to the side of the house.

Around each nail he twisted the wire, wedging a rusty barrel hoop at the bottom just so.

And just like that, a new instrument to explore.

CeDell plucked while sliding a glass bottle up and down, finding the tones between the notes.

Sweet, gliding melodies shimmied off the wire.

It wasn't the guitar he dreamed about, but it was a start.

Until . . . finally . . .

. . . a genuine six-string beauty all his own.

A Silvertone acoustic bought from a neighbor for a steal of a deal.

Now he could play like the icons on that record player:

Charley Patton. Blind Lemon Jefferson.

And—later—his hero, Robert Nighthawk.

CeDell's mother told him to stop playing that racket, but he always found a way.

He practiced out back behind the woodpile.

Or even in the outhouse.

Strumming and fretting that deep-down, stir-your-heart, rattle-your-bones blues.

The music was strong inside CeDell, but one day he felt his body growing weak.

Tired.

Aching.

He rested in the bed of a work truck in a field, longing for the end of the day.

Ten years old and scared.

When his parents brought him to the doctor, they got the diagnosis: polio.

For two long years and seven long months, CeDell stayed in the hospital.

Hour after hour, day after day, he fought for his life.

CeDell heard the blues in his head and thought about his guitar, gathering dust.

He dreamed of the day he would be home to play once again.

When CeDell finally got home, his guitar was waiting.
But try as he might, he couldn't play like he once did.
Polio had weakened his left, fretting hand.
It had stiffened his right, strumming hand.
CeDell sat in the quiet, waiting on the blues.

Sometimes music cuts like a knife.
But this time, a knife cut through the music.
CeDell had an idea.
He went straight to the silverware drawer.
To his mother's butter knives.

CeDell flipped his guitar around.

Hour after hour, day after day, CeDell discovered the way to play. *His* way.

His weakened fretting hand became a precise string-picker.

His stiffened strumming hand—now gripping the butter knife—became a smooth slide and bass-note hammer.

No one had played guitar quite like this before.

No one had sounded quite like CeDell.

CeDell played whenever and wherever he could.

Dawn to dusk to dawn again.

From street corners to the clubs.

Juke joints to house parties.

Inside. Outside.

And everywhere in between.

Chasing a trail of notes, blowin' through the breeze.

Young CeDell Davis became "Big G" Davis.

Big G: Big Guitar.

With a sound like no other. Finding tones between the notes. Using every part of that knife.

His singing voice growing as strong as his playing.

When CeDell's mother heard the depths of his talent, she told him to *keep* playing that racket.

A teenage CeDell waited for *the* Robert Nighthawk outside a radio show studio.

After a deep breath, he asked Mr. Nighthawk: Could he join his band?

"You can't play nothing," his hero said, a sly smile on his face. A friendly challenge to the young upstart.

"Wait and see," said CeDell, grinning back. Knowing.

Nighthawk called out a song for CeDell to play.

Then another.

And another again.

CeDell could play them all.

CeDell could play anything.

His way.

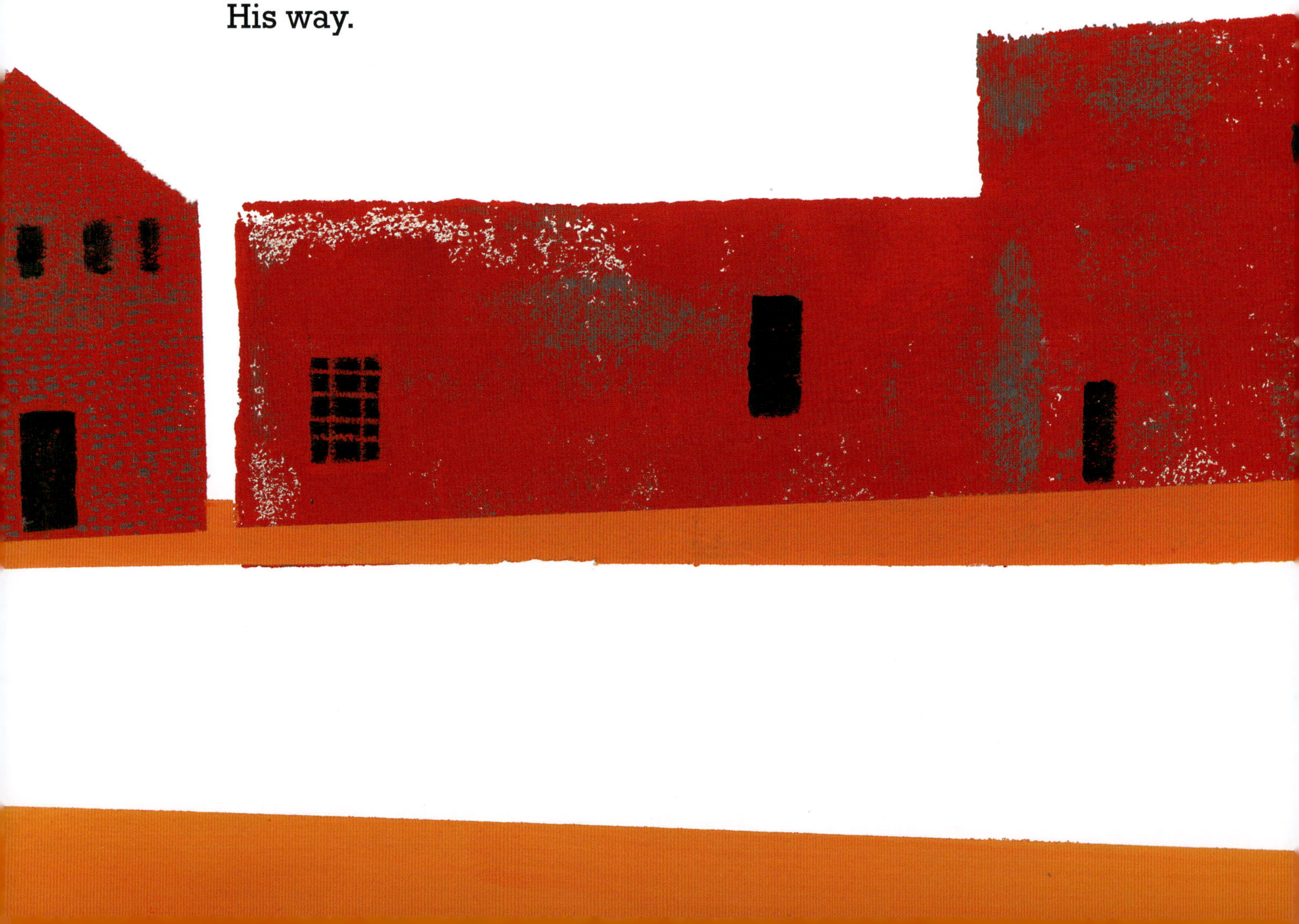

RADIO

Nothing could stop CeDell Davis.

Playing the deep-down, stir-your-heart, rattle-your-bones blues.

CeDell played with Robert Nighthawk for ten years, and with others, and out on his own.

Making a living in the juke joints and house parties, night after night.

Living in a world that was ignorant and intolerant—that was not built for him. That could be inaccessible and lonely.

He wrote songs about all of it—the ups and downs of a long and winding musical life.

A *Genuine* life with a big "G."

In his later years, a stroke took away CeDell's guitar-picking and knife-holding strength.

But it couldn't take away the music in his heart.

As the last of the original Delta bluesmen, CeDell kept singing his song.

On stage.

On the road.

And still, no one sounded quite like CeDell "Big G" Davis.

Big Greatness.

Big Gratefulness.

Big Genuineness.

Big G.

And no one ever would again.

Sometimes music cuts like a knife.
Straight to the heart.
Where it can live forever—
just like the unstoppable blues of CeDell Davis.

AUTHOR'S NOTE

Ellis CeDell "Big G" Davis was born outside Helena, Arkansas, on June 9, 1926 (sometimes reported as 1927). After his parents separated, CeDell's mother sent him and his brother to live for a time with family on the E. M. Hood sharecropping plantation near Tunica, Mississippi.

CeDell would later say in the *Blues Back Home* documentary about him that while he didn't always mind the farm work, he hated the sharecropping system he witnessed. "They'd work all the year, and at the end of the year, they didn't get nothing . . ." This corrupt cycle kept many African American tenant farmers in constant debt to landowners and restricted them from leaving, replacing slavery in all but the name. After his experience, CeDell decided he wanted to make something all his own.

Growing up in the Delta region—known as the birthplace of the blues—CeDell was surrounded by its music. His childhood friendship with Isaiah "Ike" Ross, later known as the blues musician Doctor Ross the Harmonica Boss, had a huge influence in his early musical life. Back in Helena, CeDell's father ran a grocery store/juke joint (a gathering place featuring live music, and a refuge for African Americans in the segregated south). CeDell spent time there too, reportedly sneaking in the back to see blues legends like Robert Johnson play.

CeDell contracted polio at age ten, leading to partial paralysis in his hands and legs. When he started playing guitar once again, he brought forth a whole new take on the instrument through his creativity and determination. While other guitarists also played slide with a knife, CeDell's unique skill of hitting bass notes and using every part of the knife, as well as the angle of his hand and unique tunings, created a sound all his own. Sometimes haunting. Sometimes far-out. Sometimes hardcore. But always CeDell.

It's important to note here that CeDell did not need to "overcome" his disability to play music; rather, he mastered the guitar in his own way while navigating a musical world—and a wider world—filled with barriers that needed to be broken down. Groundbreaking organizations like RAMPD (Recording Artists and Music Professionals with Disabilities) are promoting inclusion, amplifying disability culture, and advocating for visibility and accessibility within the music industry. RAMPD's movement is one that would have helped CeDell, and one that will uplift and celebrate music artists and music professionals in the industry.

After field recordings of his music by Louis Guida gained CeDell wider attention, a New York City residency with Big Joe Turner followed in the 1980s, drawing rock stars and celebrities to see him perform. *New York Times* music critic (and fellow Arkansas native) Robert Palmer wrote glowingly about his music and produced a few of his records to rave reviews and a cult following in the 1990s.

CeDell's music career seemed to be in his past once he moved into a nursing home in the mid-2000s. But a local blues musician named Greg "Big Papa" Binns and his son Zakk visited him and began jamming, with CeDell on vocals. Those visits led to a remarkable ten years of music up until the end of his life, with worldwide concerts, new albums stacked with incredible backing musicians, and a documentary honoring CeDell's life.

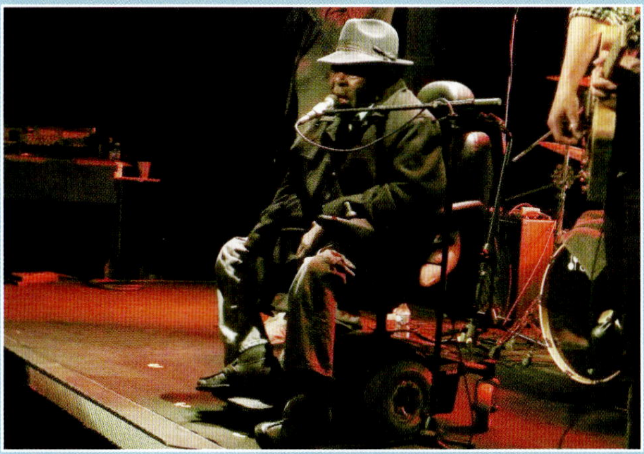

Ellis CeDell "Big G" Davis died on September 27, 2017, but his music remains as vital as ever. He is buried next to his friend and musical mentor Robert "Nighthawk" McCollum in the Magnolia Cemetery in Helena-West Helena, and the King Biscuit Blues Festival in Arkansas has a CeDell Davis Memorial Stage, where his memory—and music—live on.

CeDell Davis's 2002 record *When Lightnin' Struck the Pine* featured a backing band of R.E.M.'s Peter Buck, Screaming Trees' Barrett Martin, and other alt-rock musicians, and it was my first exposure to his story and his music. As a teen and young adult, I played guitar and bass in bands inspired by those artists, as well as the groups of the sixties and seventies that wore their blues influences on their sleeves. That album's lineup drew me in, but CeDell's distinctive playing and rich vocals made me want to dig deeper into his music—and the blues.

What I heard was nothing short of remarkable. While I was familiar with the Chicago twelve-bar blues, the spontaneity of the Delta blues it originated from was a revelation. CeDell's unmistakable tone jumped out of the speakers and grabbed me by the ear. For many music fans—myself included—it never let go. Much of the reason I wanted to write this book was to honor the musical legacy of the blues and the Black musicians who pioneered the form. I have received so much from both as a musician, and as a fan.

In the documentary *The Last Bluesman,* CeDell says, "When I'm dead and gone, people are going to be singing my songs. That's what I want." My hope is that this book will encourage readers to seek out CeDell's genuine music—and to create their own, by being themselves and bringing their own style out. Just like CeDell did.

BIBLIOGRAPHY

All quotations used in the book can be found in the following sources marked with an asterisk (*).

Baskett, Tom Jr., ed. *The Arkansas Delta: A Landscape of Change*. Helena, AR: Delta Cultural Center, 1990.

*Fettig, Tad, director. *The Last Bluesman.* Seattle: Sunyata Films/ur civilized, 2022, 1:20:43.

Gioia, Ted. *Delta Blues: The Life and Times of the Mississippi Masters Who Revolutionized American Music*. New York: W. W. Norton.

*Guida, Louis, producer. *CeDell: Blues Back Home*. Little Rock, AR: Philander Smith College, 1984.

Holden, Stephen. "CeDell Davis Offering Delta Blues Tradition." *New York Times*, May 28, 1982. nytimes.com/1982/05/28/arts/cedell-davis-offering-delta-blues-tradition.html.

Koch, Stephen. *When Lightnin' Struck the Pine,* liner notes (CeDell Davis and Friends). Recorded 2001, Fast Horse Recordings, LLC, 2002.

Martin, Barrett. *The Singing Earth: Adventures from a World of Music*. Seattle: Sunyata Books, 2017.

Palmer, Robert. "CeDell Davis," n.d. fatpossum.com/collections/cedell-davis.

———. "The Pop Life; Juke Joints: Where Styles Mate and New Music Is Born." *New York Times*, October 14, 1981. nytimes.com/1981/10/14/arts/the-pop-life-juke-joints-where-styles-mate-and-new-music-is-born.html.

Pareles, Jon. "CeDell Davis, Bluesman Who Played Guitar with a Knife, Dies at 91." *New York Times*, October 1, 2017. nytimes.com/2017/10/01/obituaries/cedell-davis-bluesman-dies.html.

Person, Barry Lee. *Highway 61*, liner notes (CeDell Davis and Herman Alexander). Recorded 1990, Wolf Records, 2003.

Phillips, Edward. "How Bluesmen Turned Their Houses into Musical Instruments (Diddley Bow 2.0)." YouTube, youtube.com/watch?v=PD4VreM8Sn4?si=EcIpm-Jme-7yLDTY.

*Ramsey, David. "Still Around Here." *Oxford American* 95, February 2, 2017. oxfordamerican.org/magazine/issue-95-winter-2016/still-around-here.

Stein, Mandy, director. *You See Me Laughin': The Last of the Hill Country Bluesmen*. New York, NY: Journeyman Pictures, 2002, 1:17.

Stolle, Roger. *Hidden History of Mississippi Blues*. Charleston, SC: History Press, 2011.

Tetreau, Jared. "Sharecropping: Slavery Rerouted." PBS, August 16, 2023. pbs.org/wgbh/americanexperience/features/harvest-sharecropping-slavery-rerouted.

Zornosa, Laura. "A New Coalition Amplifies Disability Culture in the Music Industry." *New York Times*, January 20, 2022. nytimes.com/2022/01/20/arts/music/rampd-disability-culture-music-industry.html.

ACKNOWLEDGMENTS

This book would not have been possible without the kindness of many people who took time to answer questions, search for photos, and offer encouragement. Thank you to Jimbo Mathus, whose CeDell stories at the Magnolia Cemetery I'll always treasure, and to Augusta Palmer, Gary Gazaway, Patricia Rainier, Ruthie Pride and the Delta Cultural Center, Louis Guida, Jim O'Neal, David Ramsey, Stephen Koch, John Troutman, Barrett Martin—and especially to Roger Stolle and Precious Perez for your expertise and care.

A warm thanks to Geni McCollum-Ward and Bobbie Ross for sharing about your families, and an extra-special thank you to Greg "Big Papa" Binns for your generosity of time and thoughts on the manuscript, as well your continued care and honor of Mr. Davis's legacy.

Many thanks to the incredible team at Calkins Creek, my agent Stephen Fraser for being a font of encouragement, R. Gregory Christie for bringing these words to life, as well as the SCBWI Acadiana group for keen eyes and a welcoming spirit.

Thank you to my parents for fostering my lifelong love of reading, writing, and music. To my wife, Lauren, for everything, especially your constant love and support (and always being up for a blues festival road trip), and to Savannah and Olivia for inspiration, the gift of read-alouds, and (mostly) indulging my car's CD collection.

PICTURE CREDITS

Axel Küstner: 36; Jean-Luc Martin: 37.

To my family, who makes my heart sing —*JP*

For Tom Feelings —*RGC*

Calkins Creek
An imprint of Astra Books for Young Readers,
a division of Astra Publishing House
astrapublishinghouse.com

Printed in China

ISBN: 978-1-6626-8101-1 (hc)
ISBN: 978-1-6626-8102-8 (eBook)
Library of Congress Control Number: 2025945135

First edition

10 9 8 7 6 5 4 3 2 1

Design by Melia Parsloe and Barbara Grzeslo
The text is set in Rockwell Std.
The titles are set in Linoblox Jumpy.
The illustrations are done in acrylic gouache on paper.